DEMYSTIFYING STRATEGIC PLANNING

Get more of what you want out of your business

SCOTT PATCHIN

This is a work of nonfiction.

Cover design and Layout by S.Y Lee-Wan
Editing and Publishing by Jen Hayes

ISBN: 978-1-7331346-3-7

Demystifying Strategic Planning

A workbook to help you get more of what you want out of your business.

Who this is for:

CEO, COO, Owner, CFO.

Specifically, leaders who have been frustrated with the execution of their strategic plans in the past, or who see the need for a longer-term plan but don't know where to start.

What it will do:

Clarify the terms and specifics of developing an effective strategic plan, help you understand if you could benefit from one, and show you how to lead through the gap this plan creates in your organization.

Allow you to stop wasting energy and focus on steps that will make a difference. If you need more guidance, call me.

Why I wrote this:

Too often I see leaders pursue a solution because someone they trust told them it would help – and it doesn't. The main reason this happens is because the leader did not sit back and think about WHY they need to do something different in their business.

The goal of this workbook is to help leaders name the WHY and then map out HOW they will start and WHAT specifically they will do to sustain their work until it becomes a habit.

The goal of this workbook is to help leaders name the WHY and then map out HOW they will start and WHAT specifically they will do to sustain their work until it becomes a habit.

Introduction

Strategic planning

Getting to know a new client and his or her leadership practices

Me: In my standard way of getting to know a new client and his or her leadership practices, I started our first meeting by asking, "What's your experience around strategic planning?"

Leader: He quickly pointed to a folder on the shelf above his desk and shared a story about partnering with a major university and working diligently through their process to come up with this plan.

Me: My next question was, "How have you used it, and what's been the impact?"

Leader: He shrugged and said, "I haven't opened it in a year, so I guess the simple answer is that it hasn't made an impact."

Strategic planning has been written about extensively by such reputable sources as the Harvard Business Review, the Center for Creative Leadership, and thought leaders like Jim Collins, Peter Drucker, and A.G. Lafley. With all these experts weighing in on the topic, by the time it finally gets to the leaders of organizations, I have seen it translated into a range of activities from simply defining values for the company to going on a multi-day leadership retreat.

This workbook is for leaders who have been frustrated with the execution of their strategic plans in the past, or who see the need for a longer-term plan but don't know where to start.

I have spent thousands of hours in these conversations and have discovered it's most important to begin by getting on the same page around three questions:

1. How do you know you need a strategic plan?
2. What actually is a strategic plan?
3. What are the key outcomes of an effective strategic plan?

We'll look at each question in turn.

Question 1:

How do I know I need a strategic plan?

One of my core beliefs is that great conversations start with a question.

In my book, ***People-Centered Performance: Bringing out our best through honest conversations,*** I share my core belief that great conversations start with a question. Applying that here, leaders will tell you their needs based on the frustrations they share and the questions they ask.

Here are some of the most common questions I hear from leaders needing a plan:

- I'm tired of working late to deal with the issues while my team leaves on time. How do I fix that?
- Our sales have been flat for three years, even though our market is growing. What do you do that will address that?
- When I'm gone, my leadership team fails to meet and delays decisions until I return. What is wrong with them?
- I keep telling people what they need to do to save money and they never follow through. Do I have the right people?
- Most of our sales come from one or two customers, and I am getting nervous because sales are slowing. How do I fix that?
- I keep trying to spend more time away from work to test what retirement will look like, and I always have to come back and fix things. How do I make things less dependent on me so I can actually take longer breaks?

Have you said or felt any of these things? Each of these can be translated into the simple statement, "I need a strategic plan."

Most leaders I work with are so focused on the work at hand that they don't hear themselves making these statements repeatedly. An effective way to listen to yourself is to ask input from those around you. Ask your spouse, children, or close friends what they hear you complain about most. If it aligns with any of the above statements, a plan is needed.

A second area to inspect for yourself is the clarity of your team around the handful of priorities the business needs to accomplish. Achieving these priorities will take teamwork, which can only happen if everyone has absolute clarity around the plan and maintains that clarity and focus throughout their work.

Here are three quick statements to test this:

- My team can name the top three to five priorities for this year. (I challenge you to test this by having everyone independently write these down on a piece of paper and then hand them in.)

- The whole team reviews our progress toward reaching our yearly goals at least once per month.

- We hit our key financial and organizational goals last year.

Here is a story to illustrate the current condition of most teams around the first statement, which tests a team's alignment on priorities:

> I had a chance to watch Brian Bagley, a senior member of the research team for ***Good to Great,*** facilitate a session with senior leaders from a Fortune 100 company. During his first activity, he asked each person to write down the top three strategies for their organization. When they had all been shared, there were eleven different answers.
>
> This points to the importance and challenge of being able to answer YES to the statement, "My team can name the top three to five priorities for this year."

If you answer NO to either statement two or three, your issue is around execution not planning. This translates into examining your leadership team and how the work is divided up, reviewing how often you are talking about strategy and priorities together, and focusing on your effectiveness as a leader.

In my article around the key gaps that leaders need to master, ***Don't Avoid Gaps, Lead Through Them,*** I framed strategic planning as the leadership team's work of creating a gap for the organization to overcome. A key goal of strategic planning is the intentional creation of a picture of the current state and the desired future state for the business.

By using these three statements to assess your current condition around frustrations and performance, you can determine if developing a plan and the management discipline to use it will provide a greater ROTI (Return On Time Invested) for you and your leadership team.

What is a gap?

A gap is the space between where we are and where we want to go. Sometimes it's as simple as stepping onto a subway car, but in business it becomes a complex exercise to determine precisely what your current state is and to use some of those same measures to define a future state.

Make Your Action Plan

Listen to Yourself

Ask input from those around you. Here's what they hear you say:

Listen to Your Team

Ask each member of your team to write down the top three to five priorities for the business this year and hand them in. What do you find?

Look back at your schedule over the past 6 months – how often is the whole team reviewing progress toward reaching yearly goals? This should happen at least once per month.

Look back at last year's results – did you hit your key financial and organizational goals?

Question 2:

What actually is a strategic plan?

(including key terms used during the process)

The fundamental goal and outcome of a strategic plan is to create a performance gap for the organization that will be bridged through the ongoing work of a healthy and smart leadership team.

Before having a conversation around strategic planning, we must first establish alignment around the terms we use during the process. These terms describe the pieces that create a great plan and the management practices that create a strong culture of accountability around the plan so things get done!

My experience is in helping teams use a complete and proven system called EOS® or Entrepreneurial Operating System®, so some of the terms I use are specific to that system. However, I also provide descriptions of each that will help you establish quick connections with other systems you might use because the same pieces are present in any planning system. If you want to know more about EOS, I provide a link at the end to explore it further.

Earlier, I introduced the concept of gaps. It is an important concept to repeat here:

The fundamental goal and outcome of a strategic plan is to create a performance gap for the organization that will be bridged through the ongoing work of a healthy and smart leadership team.

Here are the five pieces that need to be present in a strategic plan:

1. Vision:
A clear definition of the gap you are creating for the business – including any actions that need to be taken such as gathering data to confirm or challenge your assumptions.

2. Clear assumptions that were used in defining the gap:
These are defined by values, mission statement, a description of your target market, the three things that make your product or service unique in the marketplace, and a process that defines the customer experience. I call these assumptions because they are clear things you believe or know about your core business and culture that everyone needs to agree on. There are a handful of these things that need to be documented during the process.

3. Operational Plan / Tactical Plan:
A shorter-term plan (next 90 days and next 12 months) to focus the efforts of the organization on closing the gap; this gives the plan clarity and focus for the team to execute now. Typically, this happens once your goals are set, and the most effective companies break that down further into things that need to get done in the next month or quarter. In EOS®, we call this part Traction®; Stephen Covey introduced the term Rocks for these shorter-term priorities, which is a great word to use in this case.

4. Scorecard / KPI / Dashboard:
Clear measures of success you will use to assess progress in closing the gap. The key time periods in which to measure performance are weekly, monthly, quarterly, and annually. One of the realities that Gino Wickman addresses in EOS is that more frequent viewing of the critical measures is essential. Gino found that it is most critical for the leadership team to create a scorecard of seven to fifteen measures which are reviewed weekly. This gives the leaders a pulse of the business and ties back to the timeless bit of wisdom: ***you must inspect what you expect.*** Running your business on data and developing the discipline to look at it often and together has the impact of making decisions easier to understand because they become more objective rather than subjective or emotion based.

5. Organizational Assessment:
What structure and skills/experience do you need to close this gap with your work? Using a phrase Jim Collins made famous, "Do you have the right people in the right seats?" The tougher question leaders need to ask, and have the courage to be honest answering is, "Are you the right leader?"

The strategic plan contains all the information for your organization around these five pieces.

The three key gaps leaders need to create and manage within their organization:

Gap #1:
Creating a performance gap for your organization
(aka, strategic planning)

Gap #2:
Developing the detailed plan to close the gap created by the strategic plan, and the work to manage the plan to completion
(aka, operational or tactical planning)

Gap #3:
Managing the individual performance gap created by the previous two steps
(aka, leadership or individual development)

There are some key terms here that need to be standardized so as not to cause confusion.

Vision without traction is hallucination.
Gino Wickman, Traction: Get a Grip on Your Business

Vision – The longer-term, less tangible parts of the plan:

Within the plan, there are longer-term elements that may or may not relate directly to a defined point of success but serve as filters to make good decisions for the business. These are often collectively called the vision. Typically, the vision piece contains the following items:

- **Values:**
  Core beliefs about how to treat people and what is important. This is the DNA of your organization.

- **Mission Statement:**
  The purpose, cause, or passion of your organization. This is the reason you come to work.

- **BHAGs (Big Hairy Audacious Goals):**
  A term created by Jim Collins, this is a longer-term goal focused on stretching how you as a leader think about the future state of your business. It is supposed to energize and overwhelm, so you step back and work on scaling what you have.

- **Target Market:**
  Three to seven statements that define who your ideal customer is in terms of where they are, how they think, and what they care about.

- **Three Uniques / Niche:**
  What do you do best? What differentiates your offering from others?

- **Three-Year Picture™:**
  This is an EOS® term for the picture our plan is trying to make happen. It is also referred to as the vivid picture and is essentially the outcomes you envision for your organization. This includes numbers, specific achievements, physical location/surroundings, and feelings that you and your team are experiencing at a certain date 2-5 years into the future.

Operational Plan / Tactical Plan – The shorter-term (90 days to 1 year) part of the plan:

This provides specific measures, actions, priorities, and owners for the work, which all must happen to move the organization toward the longer-term goals. This short-term plan is called the tactical or operational plan, and typically contains the following:

- **Yearly Goals:**
  The three to seven significant things that will be accomplished in the next 12 months. Less is more.

- **Scorecard:**
  Sometimes referred to as KPIs (key performance indicators), dashboard, or metrics. This pulls in measures from all parts of the organization so the health of the business can be accurately assessed in a timely manner.

- **Rocks:**
  Your shorter-term goals (typically 90 days) that need to be accomplished by individuals to help make progress toward yearly goals (credit goes to Stephen Covey and his analogy around rocks, gravel, sand, and water – search for a YouTube video on this if you would like to learn more).

Strategy without tactics is the slowest route to victory. Tactics without strategy is the noise before defeat.

Sun Tzu

Organizational Assessment – Critically looking at your structure and people:

This is about reviewing the leadership and talents you need to effectively execute your plan. An organizational assessment typically contains the following:

- **Accountability Chart™:**
  This is an EOS®-specific term that refers to the roles and structure you need to execute this plan; some organizations use a different tool called an organizational chart.

- **Clear leadership standards / expectations:**
  This is the foundation for answering the question – How is our leadership team performing as a team? How you will lead (your standards) is as important as your business goals if culture matters in your organization. This also gives a lens to each leader to understand what they need to do to become a more effective leader.

- **Assessing each role / individual:**
  Clear performance expectations are the first step, and the next step has to be – Do I have the right people for the seats (roles and structure) and are they in the right place to accomplish the work defined by our plan?

Having a plan is critical, but not having the right people in place to execute it will ultimately lead to a plan that does not work. When it seems that something is not working, most of us just stop doing it. If you have had plans fail in the past, step back and ask yourself which part you skipped? In my experience, it is usually related to what Jim Collins called 'the right people in the right seats' conversations.

The executives who ignited the transformations from good to great did not first figure out where to drive the bus and then get people to take it there. No, they first got the right people on the bus (and the wrong people off the bus) and then figured out where to drive it.
They said, in essence,
'Look, I don't really know where we should take this bus. But I know this much:
If we get the right people on the bus,
the right people in the right seats, and the wrong people off the bus, then we'll figure out how to take it someplace great.'

Jim Collins,
Good to Great

Make Your Action Plan

Create a Vision: Tips for getting started

1. Pick a date 5 or 10 years in the future. What is the one goal you have for your organization?

Tip: This could be a BHAG (something that will stretch you, even scare you) or it could be a key focus area that the organization needs to work toward to stay ahead of your competition.

2. This idea is shared by Rich Sheridan in his book ***Joy, Inc: How We Built a Workplace People Love.*** It can be done individually to help you think bigger, or it can be an activity where partners work independently then come together to share their stories. Here is how Rich describes it: "Take a quiet hour to sit down with your computer, tablet, or a pen and paper and describe a good day 5 years from now. Pick an exact day. Write down what is happening in your life and in the life of the company on that day. The opening line is – It's June 1, 20XX, and today I..." (p. 241)

3. Pick an end-of-year date 3 years from now and describe your company in two different ways. First, pick a sales number, a profit number, and a few other metrics that describe what your organization has achieved. Second, in a series of bulleted statements, describe what your organization looks like. What are you celebrating? Who is celebrating with you? What do your facilities look like? What do your products/services look like? What does your culture feel like? What are your people saying about your organization? *In EOS®, this is something we refer to as the Three-Year Picture™. If you want to learn more, read the detailed description in the book ***Traction*** by Gino Wickman that I referenced earlier.

Date: ________________

Sales: ________________

Profit: ________________

Question 2: What actually is a strategic plan?

Other measures:

What does it look like?

-
-
-
-
-
-
-
-
-
-
-
-
-
-
-
-
-
-
-
-
-
-

Make Your Action Plan

Develop an Operational Plan / Tactical Plan: The shorter-term (90 days to 1 year) part of the plan. There are two parts to this. The first is the goals for the year, and the second the shorter-term projects (or rocks) that you will complete in the next 90 days.

1. Plan for the year: Pick a date 1 year in the future. Typically, it is the end of your financial year to align reporting. Define the measures you will use and a handful of goals for the year. Remember: with goals, less is more!

   Date: ____________

   Sales: ___________

   Profit: ___________

   Other measures:

   Goal 1:

   Goal 2:

   Goal 3:

   Goal 4:

Tips: Remember to make each goal SMART. One of the keys to doing that is defining what success or done will look like for each goal. There is a worksheet to help you make goals SMART-Er at the end of the next section.

Question 2: What actually is a strategic plan?

---

2. Plan for next 90 days: What are the immediate things that need to get done over the next 90 days to help you work toward your plan for the year? Pick a date 90 days in the future, define your key measures, and define a handful of shorter-term projects/rocks that need to get completed. Each of these should have a single owner that will drive the work and be ready to report on the status at team meetings.

   Date: ________________

   Sales: ________________

   Profit: ________________

   Other measures:

   Rock/Project 1:

   Rock/Project 2:

   Rock/Project 3:

   Rock/Project 4:

Finally, pick a meeting where these projects will be reported on and discussed if any fall behind schedule for completion by the desired date. This meeting should ideally be weekly, and all owners of the projects/rocks must be present. Never go longer than two weeks between reviewing the progress toward these goals.

Make Your Action Plan

Questions to ask yourself

Complete an Organizational Assessment: Critically looking at your structure and people

This is the most complex topic to try and simplify so you can get started.
The simple question you have to first answer:

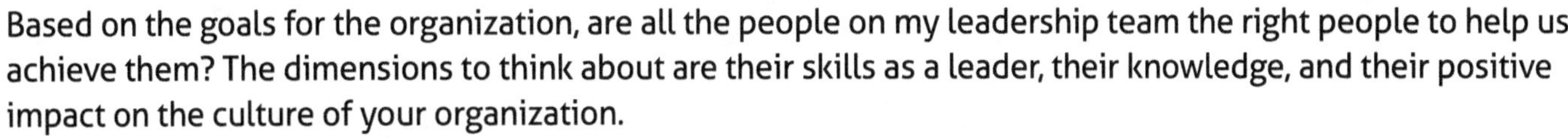

Based on the goals for the organization, are all the people on my leadership team the right people to help us achieve them? The dimensions to think about are their skills as a leader, their knowledge, and their positive impact on the culture of your organization.

I highly recommend you read about the People Component of EOS®. It is described in detail in chapter 4 of the book Traction by Gino Wickman. It is the simplest way I have found to answer this question.

You can use the worksheet here to outline your thoughts:

My Leadership Team

1. ______________________________

Skills:

Knowledge:

Positive impact:

2. ______________________________

Skills:

Knowledge:

Positive impact:

My Leadership Team

3. ______________________

Skills:

Knowledge:

Positive impact:

---

4. ______________________

Skills:

Knowledge:

Positive impact:

---

5. ______________________

Skills:

Knowledge:

Positive impact:

My Leadership Team

6. ______________________________

Skills:

Knowledge:

Positive impact:

---

7. ______________________________

Skills:

Knowledge:

Positive impact:

---

8. ______________________________

Skills:

Knowledge:

Positive impact:

Question 3:

What are the key outcomes of an effective strategic plan?

There are three key outcomes you will achieve with an effective strategic plan.

Key Outcome #1: More of what you want out of your business

The most common assumption people make is that planning is about more profit. That can be true, but my experience working with entrepreneurs and entrepreneurial leadership teams has taught me that profit is not always the answer to this question.

Here are some other frequent answers I have heard from leaders:

- **Control**
- **Time**
- **Sustainability**

Myth: Leaders hold people accountable.

Truth: Leaders create conditions where accountability happens through the actions and ownership of their team.

Here are some simple (but not easy) steps that will help you start establishing a culture of accountability:

- As a team, create longer-term goals (3-12 months) for the organization.
- Translate the goals into monthly and weekly work for your leaders and their teams.
- Clearly define measures and/or outcomes for the work so that performance expectations are crystal clear. A helpful tool is the SMART methodology. There is a worksheet to help you make your goals SMART-Er at the end of this section.
- Meet weekly as a team to review progress, and quickly handle any issues that are impeding the progress of people completing the work they committed to.
- Leaders: Trust your teammates by asking for help when you need it and not being afraid to have conflict around critical decisions. This point leads us to key outcome #2.

Key Outcome #2: Stronger and healthier leadership team

One of the biggest barriers to planning is time. Leaders of growth-minded organizations often feel they don't have time to leave the business to learn. I hear this often as teams contemplate the ROI of planning.

I maintain a belief that has been reinforced by my work – an effective strategic planning process creates a leadership development class in your business. As leaders work IN and ON the business, they will be challenged and supported to become more effective leaders as they do their work.

The critical elements to learning as you lead are:

- A clear picture of the gap/work that needs to get done.
- A conversation to ensure each leader is in the right role for their strengths, passions, and rewards; this takes away the issue that we are asking them to do work they are not capable of successfully completing.
- Feedback on what support is needed for each leader to complete the work.
- **TRUST** within the team and **TRUTH** from the team, so that timely feedback is provided; the secret is each leader identifying successes and failures quickly so a dynamic environment does not get in the way of completing the work.

Changes will happen. Trust, truth, and resilience are the secret ingredients to completing the work in spite of that change.

Scott Patchin

Key Outcome #3: You start leading more and doing less

This may sound obvious, but the number one reason organizations don't grow is because the leader or leaders will not delegate work. I use a definition of leadership created by Ken Blanchard – "Leadership is an influence process. It is working with people to accomplish their goals and the goals of the organization."

Leadership is an influence process. It is working with people to accomplish their goals and the goals of the organization.

Ken Blanchard

The critical first step for a leader is not creating the plan. It is creating the conditions within the team where planning and execution can happen. There are critical steps in creating these conditions.

Here are a few tips to assess your own capacity to lead, and the current health of your team/organization:

- **Look in the mirror:** Any issues your organization has with planning and executing that plan reflect your leadership style. To get a different outcome, you will have to change and make some difficult decisions. Do you accept that responsibility and are you willing to change to lead more and tell less?

- **Do you have the patience to make it a conversation?** A conversation means that there is a balance of talking and listening. Really powerful conversations require some 'thinking and doing time' between them. If strategic planning is seen as a single event rather than a process in your organization, it is not going to have the intended impact.

- **Are you willing to do the hard work of making sure you have the right people on your team?** It takes focus on which leadership roles you need in your organization to be successful, then how the people you have today fit into those roles. If there is not an acceptable fit or you do not have the confidence in a leader to learn fast enough to perform a role, do not put them in it. In my experience, it is more painful to remove someone than to deny someone for very tangible reasons.

The existence of trust does not necessarily mean they like one another, it means they understand one another.

Peter Drucker

- **Insist on TRUST and TRANSPARENCY from the beginning – and you go first as the leader:** Whenever I ask people if they use a trust-giving or trust-earning approach to new relationships, the breakdown is usually around 50/50. A famous quote on this topic is, "Trust, but verify." The modification I would add is, "Trust – Support and/or ask for help – Verify – Repeat." As soon as you drop the TRUST piece for your peers, or you lose the TRUST piece from your peers, the work becomes a lot harder and your teams will begin to emulate the relationships they see on the executive team.

Make Your Action Plan

Get More of What You Want

What are the top three things you would like to change about your business or get more of within your business?

1.

2.

3.

Learning as You Lead

Do you have a clear picture of the gap/work that needs to get done? Define it here:

Have you had the appropriate conversations to ensure each leader is in the right role for their strengths, passions, and rewards? Outline any changes here:

Have you asked for feedback on what support is needed for each leader to complete the work? Start listing here (and use additional pages as needed):

How will you ensure each leader is identifying successes and failures quickly, so a dynamic environment does not get in the way of completing the work?

Make Your Action Plan

Assessing Your Capacity to Lead

Any issues your organization has with planning and executing that plan reflect your leadership style.
To get a different outcome, you will have to change and make some difficult decisions.
Do you accept that responsibility and are you willing to change to lead more and tell less?

Do you have the patience to make it a conversation?
A conversation means that there is a balance of talking and listening.
Really powerful conversations require some 'thinking and doing time' between them.

Are you willing to do the hard work of making sure you have the right people on your team?
It takes focus on which leadership roles you need in your organization to be successful, then how the people you have today fit into those roles. If there is not an acceptable fit or you do not have the confidence in a leader to learn fast enough to perform a role, do not put them in it. In my experience, it is more painful to remove someone than to deny someone for very tangible reasons.

Do you have the persistence to insist on **TRUST** and **TRANSPARENCY** from the beginning – and are you willing to go first as the leader? Remember, "Trust – Support and/or ask for help – Verify – Repeat."

Make Your Action Plan

SMART Methodology – Making Your Goal SMART-Er

SMART goals are Specific, Measurable, Achievable, Results-oriented, and Time-bound. The E asks you to look at yourself and how you feel about your goal (hint: this is key!).
Use the following questions to refine your goals into actionable steps that can be measured and managed.
Write your goal here:

Specific

Too often we speak in general terms because it is safer and easier. We are also challenged to think BIG, and our goals (sometimes called BHAG or Stretch goals) reflect that. Terms like ***always*** or ***everyone*** provide a general idea of what we want to do, but the details stay in our own head.

Problem: Nobody else knows what we mean, and a critical part of accomplishing a goal is enlisting the support of others. Making a goal more specific gives others a greater ability to help us. Naming a person or a behavior that we are trying to change also helps us focus on a behavior or a person that matters.

Here are four questions to help you reframe your goal to make it more specific:

1. What situation/experience was I thinking about when I wrote this goal?

2. Who was I thinking about when I wrote this goal?

3. What behavior/situation am I going to positively impact with this goal?

4. What action am I going to take?

Based on your answers to the previous questions, rewrite your goal below to make it more **specific:**

Question 3: What are the key outcomes of an effective strategic plan?

Measurable

It could be a specific measure, it could be feedback from others, or it could be our own internal measure. Regardless of what you choose, it is important to give some indication of what success looks like if you accomplish this goal.

Problem: In ***Good to Great***, Jim Collins talked about the Flywheel Effect for organizations and the importance and energy-giving effect of achieving a goal. Not having a goal takes away the opportunity to celebrate.

Here are three questions to help you reframe your goal and define an outcome (this could be adding an extra sentence; don't feel like all goals have to be a single sentence):

1. What does success look like when I achieve this goal?

2. What outcome do those impacted the most by my shift define as a desired outcome?

3. What outcome am I committing to?

Based on your answers to the previous questions, rewrite your goal below to make it more **measurable:**

Achievable

People get busy, and it is important to set goals that can be completed quickly and create momentum toward a bigger goal.

Problem: When we make a goal targeted at a whole team, or every relationship we have, or our top 5 customers it results in a goal that could take 6 months or a year to complete. Success fuels success, so it is important to make it achievable by focusing on impacting ONE thing over the next 30 days. Again, there could be multiple goals/actions to achieve something bigger and working in 30-day blocks of time will keep the focus on moving forward.

Here are several questions to help you reframe your goal to make it more achievable:

1. How long will it take to achieve my goal?
2. Is my goal focused on a single person, habit, or customer?
3. If not, who/what will be the single focus of my efforts?
4. Is it realistic to think that I can achieve this in 30 days?
   (If yes, skip to rewriting the goal. If no, go to next question.)
5. What can I achieve in the next 7-30 days?
   (Remember, it takes 21 days of practice to change a SINGLE habit.)

Based on your answers to the previous questions, rewrite your goal below to make it more **achievable:**

Results-oriented

This is similar to measurable. The unique part is it must be strongly supported by others as being a desired result.

Problem: When we measure things without thinking about maximizing the impact on the business or team, we risk hitting a goal that will not have a significant impact on the business.

Here are three questions to help you reframe your goal to have maximum impact on your business:

1. What overall business goals will this impact?
   If the answer is NONE – What measure will it impact that SHOULD be embraced by the overall business?

2. Do I need the support of anyone else to achieve this goal?

3. If needed – What would have to change about this goal to make the result have the impact it should?

Based on your answers to the previous questions, rewrite your goal below to make it more **results-oriented:**

Time-bound

This builds off the measurable piece by assigning a specific date when the commitment will be completed.

Problem: When leaders are not having one-on-ones at least monthly with their people, it creates a vacuum where goals set are not revisited often enough. It is important to assign a date to everything so problems can be identified sooner and/or everyone is in the habit of ongoing celebrations of success.

Here are two questions to help you reframe your goal to make it targeted by a specific date:

1. What date will I achieve this goal?

2. Is the date < 30 days out?
   If yes, when will I review it with my leader? If no, return to the achievable step.

Based on your answers to the previous questions, rewrite your goal below to make it more **time-bound**

Excited

Are you EXCITED about achieving this goal?

Work does not always have to be fun and exciting, but when it is special things happen. ***Passion is the secret sauce of performance*** and being intentional about tapping into it is the extra step to this process.

Problem: We all get into ruts where we go through the motions. Life happens, and it is unrealistic to believe that every goal will be something that the pursuit of actually generates energy within us. However, what if we could make little changes to our goals that would increase our energy generators by 10%?

Here are two questions to help you reframe your goal to make it something you can get excited about:

1. On a scale of 1 (not excited) to 10 (extremely excited), what is my level of excitement about this goal?

2 If < 8, what would it take to make it an 8+?

Based on your answers to the previous questions, rewrite your goal to make it more desirable.
If you rated it an 8 or above, you are already done!

Final Goal:

Embrace the concept

Failure teaches

In a past role, I was charged with developing leaders for mortgage operations to set up in different states. As part of the 7-month leadership development program, each candidate spent 6-8 weeks in our collections operations. The reason for this was based in the belief that to write a good loan meant understanding what happened when loans did not get paid. Seeing and experiencing failure was the only way to really learn this lesson. With that knowledge, the work of the underwriters became easier to understand because the leaders were equipped to manage the risk. The result was a greater trust in the underwriters and the underwriting process, and an increase in the sales team's ability to identify and present a good deal.

It's important to consider why strategic plans fail so you can better understand how to create a robust one. Here we look at five of the most common reasons this happens and what you can do to avoid it.

A key question that every leader needs to know the answer to is, "Why do strategic plans fail?"

Researchers Donald Sull, Rebecca Homkes, and Charles Sull published ***Why Strategy Execution Unravels – and What to Do About It*** in the March 2015 edition of the Harvard Business Review. Here are the five reasons they found that plans fail, presented as myths that doom the process of executing a strategy:

Myth #1: Execution Equals Alignment
In my terms, the easy part is having the spreadsheet that connects corporate goals to departmental goals and then to individual goals. What dooms the execution of a plan is departments actually working together ***(i.e., teamwork)*** because of lack of trust between the leaders. That relationship translates into a barrier to effectively executing the strategy.

Myth #2: Execution Means Sticking to the Plan
A key term here is 'agility', which translates into the discipline and habits of the leadership team to monitor progress and make changes to the plan/priorities when certain conditions require it. Agility does not mean change all the time, but it does mean change when something needs to change. Your role as a leader and a leadership team becomes difficult and important here, because you have to develop an understanding of when to change the plan and when to stick to the plan.

Myth #3: Communication Equals Understanding

One of my core phrases with leaders is that great conversations start with a question. Too often leaders define 'communication' by the organization of what they say and ***not*** by how effectively the message is understood at all levels of the organization. Understanding can be evidenced by answering questions, asking individuals to repeat back what they understand, and taking action based on a clear understanding of the core messages.

Myth #4: A Performance Culture Drives Execution

I remember a succession planning conversation where a CFO brought in her list of high performers based on their P&L performance from the previous two years. Quickly, the human resources leader weighed in that two of those leaders received the worst employee engagement scores, and their operations had not generated any meaningful future leaders to the company since they took over as leaders. This story illustrates the key to this issue – that performance is multi-faceted. It is important to measure performance by ***what*** is accomplished and ***how*** it is accomplished. Rewarding things like agility, teamwork, and ambition – and mentoring future leaders – helps create a more balanced definition for 'performance culture'.

Myth #5: Execution Should Be Driven from the Top

This is probably the most important point, because thought leaders like Jack Welch and Larry Bossidy have written books that provide a glimpse into their styles which can easily be interpreted as CEO-driven strategy. The research points to the concept that 'distributed leaders' actually drive the strategy, while executive leaders need to guide it through their actions. This enables key decisions to be made in a timely fashion, while any issues that are holding up execution quickly get elevated, discussed, and solved.

Next Steps

Where do I start?

Great conversations start with a question, so I recommend answering these three questions first. I would also encourage you to ask two or three trusted advisors or team members to answer the same questions:

1. What is the gap I see in this business?

2. How committed am I to bringing a group of people together to close it?

3. What is my confidence in the leaders' capacity to close the gap?

If your answers to these questions indicate a desire for growth and a commitment to developing a team of leaders capable of managing that growth, then a strategic plan is a logical next step.

Now you need to get to work. First, educate yourself on the key aspects of the strategic plan. Next, select an approach you will use to create a vision for your organization, identify specific goals for the next year and rocks for the next 90 days, and develop a defined schedule for your leadership team to revisit and revise the plan.

If you are overwhelmed at the thought of making some of the changes I have talked about, you are not alone. Here are some additional materials that will give you more background information to help you build your own planning process. I have also included some EOS®-specific learning based on a system created by Gino Wickman that I have mentioned several times. I have found EOS to be a very effective tool for helping entrepreneurial leaders and leadership teams, so much so that it is now the only tool I use.

Here are two books that will help you learn more and a link to the EOS website:

- ***Traction: Get a Grip on Your Business*** by Gino Wickman
- If you would like to read a story version of the EOS process, I recommend ***Get a Grip: How to Get Everything You Want from Your Entrepreneurial Business*** by Gino Wickman and Mike Paton
- Website with more information: **eosworldwide.com**

Here are some books and articles for those of you looking to create or improve your own planning process:

- ***Can You Say What Your Strategy Is?*** by David J. Collis and Michael G. Rukstad (Harvard Business Review)
- ***Building Your Company's Vision*** by James C. Collins and Jerry I. Porras (Harvard Business Review)
- ***Scaling Up*** by Verne Harnish
- ***Predictable Success*** by Les McKeown
- ***The Great Game of Business*** by Jack Stack

Expanded reading list for becoming proficient in understanding strategic planning and how to effectively lead it:

- ***Why Strategy Execution Unravels and What to Do About It*** by Donald Sull, Rebecca Homkes, and Charles Sull (Harvard Business Review)
- ***Good to Great*** by Jim Collins
- ***Joy, Inc.: How We Built a Workplace People Love*** by Richard Sheridan
- ***A Lapsed Anarchist's Approach to Building a Great Business*** by Ari Weinzweig

I like to use the word journey when thinking about strategic planning because of the simple definition: ***an act of traveling from one place to another.*** We have all been on journeys and know that the significant journeys we take are not straight paths, but are fraught with twists, turns, changes, and surprises. Because of this, I would like to make one additional offer to help you on your journey:

- Contact me for a free one-hour conversation to explore this journey. I have considerable experience in growth and a well-developed network of resources, and I am willing to share both once we decide what you need. You can contact me through **thetrugroup.com/eosjourney/**

Strategic planning is a journey - an act of traveling from one place to another. We have all been on journeys and know that the significant journeys we take are not straight paths, but are fraught with twists, turns, changes, and surprises.

I will leave you with one final quote that captures the importance of the strategic planning process for you as the CEO, Entrepreneur, Founder, or whatever role you played in growing your business to this point:

If you want to go FAST, go ALONE.
If you want to go FAR, go TOGETHER.

African Proverb

The part I would add –
Effective strategic planning is about going FASTER and FARTHER
~ TOGETHER.

More about TrUst and TrUth from Scott

When I launched my consulting business in 2009, I became that consultant across the table from leaders. I was faced with posing the big questions: "What problem are you trying to solve?" and "What's keeping you up at night?" I found that leaders tend to identify problems clustered around their perceived needs, rather than asking how to improve their own leadership capabilities.

From my two decades of working with leaders and studying leadership, two truths have emerged:

1. If your leadership journey is driven by the latest book, you will end up spending too much time chasing someone else's vision of leadership.

2. The most effective form of leadership development follows the formula: LEARNING + DOING = GROWTH.

With this epiphany, I defined one of my foundational philosophies of leadership and put it into my company's name. This two-pronged precept is central to the underlying philosophy, and name, of The trU Group; specifically, that the two things leaders must work at every day are building trUst – between the leader and the team, as well as within the team – and leveraging that trUst to get the trUth, in all its forms, on the table. (The 'U' is capitalized because, as a leader, for trust to exist and truth to emerge, you must first focus on 'U'. I firmly believe that being a people-centered leader is essential to effective servant leadership.)

The two things leaders must work at every day are building trUst and leveraging that trUst to get the trUth on the table - first focusing on 'U'.

Q&A

Questions Leaders Often Ask

Q: What if I lead a business group that depends on creating a strategy that aligns with a larger organizational strategy?

A: First, the only difference is that the environment you operate in is mostly defined by the internal business customers you have. So the process is the same, and you start by asking the same critical questions about what gaps you see and how committed you are to closing those gaps. The easy way is to create no strategy, point to the lack of leadership in your organization, and focus on managing the day-to-day pieces of your business. If you want to create a strategy, read the articles mentioned here. Then go gather the critical information you need from your customers to plan for the next year.

Q: How do I gather important information from my customers for our planning process?

A: The short answer, ask. If there is time, your customers' perspective is incredibly helpful – especially when trying to create shorter-term plans to address issues in your current business or if your strategy involves finding more of the right customers. Some questions to ask:

- What are the two to three key challenges facing your business over the next 12 months?
- In thinking about your business, and going out 12 months and looking back, what does success look like?
- How do you measure success for the services we provide you?
- What would you say are the key reasons you continue to be our customer?

Q: Leadership matters. But what is it?

A: Every leader I talk to, at any level of an organization, agrees on one thing: leadership is critical for the success of an organization. It makes or breaks us, individually and collectively, and we've all had firsthand experience with leaders who either brought out the best or worst in everyone around them.

But why? While we can all agree on how important effective leadership is, I find little agreement or clarity on how to achieve it. Far too often, the path to good leadership is defined by the consultant sitting in front of you. Leadership training has become a multi-billion-dollar business, resulting in leaders following the latest book or fad. In fact, a simple Amazon search for books on leadership today yields more than 175,000 choices! No wonder leaders feel overwhelmed by conflicting advice.

I always encourage leaders to define for themselves what they think leadership is, then ask them to use the training they receive to refine their own definition. This workbook is about helping you, as a leader, develop your understanding of what effective leadership looks like and how it translates into developing the people around you, who are critical to your success.

Your Planning Framework

The Honest Culture Journey

Plans help leaders move the organization, but being involved in the planning is the key step in getting the 21st century team member to own it and drive it. If you want extra passion and effort, include them!

Scott Patchin

Strategic planning is a journey. Using the lens of honest culture to manage it will make the outcomes so much more powerful and the journey so much more energizing.

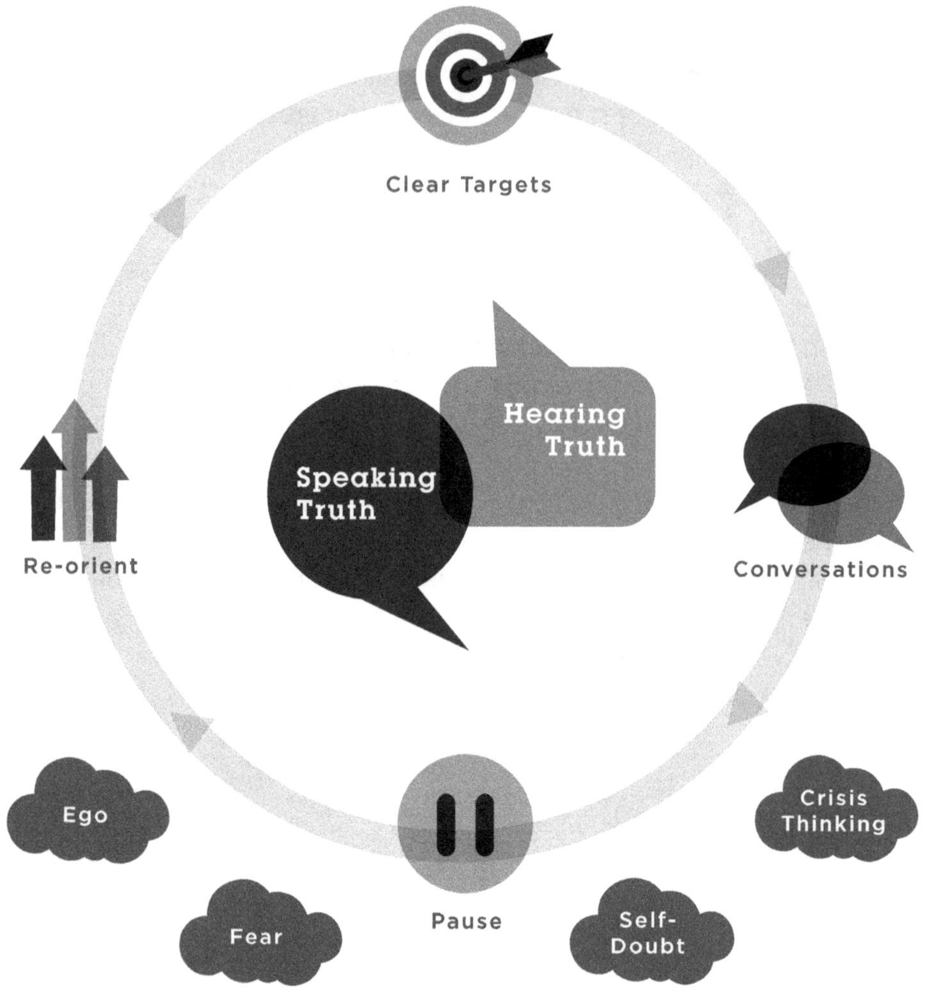

The center of the Honest Culture Journey is speaking truth and hearing truth. This is at the heart of the work. To the extent it happens, the journey becomes a place where respect is given and felt, which is a key ingredient to a healthy and high-performing team. Trust and respect are accelerators to success.

To get you started, here is how the key events go together:

Clear Targets

Every journey has a destination – whether it is physical, spiritual, or emotional. There is always a reason. When a team is involved, it provides the foundation for the relationships from the very beginning. It starts with the simple question: "Why are we doing this?" Then it gets to the other key pieces of information – the who? what? where? when? and how? of our journey. There are two more key questions to answer, but this gets us started.

Conversations

Our journey joins the need to achieve something and the relationship outcome of doing it as a team. This step is about all the interactions that just happen when we journey together. Things like same room/same time connections, instant texts or emails, or even slow connections such as dangling texts, unresolved emails, or other barriers to our sense of immediacy.

Pause

Journeys are fraught with movement, emotions, shortages, and lots of rerouting. The pause is an intentional event to slow down and focus people on speaking truth and, even more importantly, hearing truth. It can be a one-to-one, leader-to-many, or a team pause (three to eight people). There is no time limit, only the objective to quiet the noise of the journey to speak and hear truth from each other. An effective pause creates an emotionally safe place for all to share and a physical space to allow all to focus.

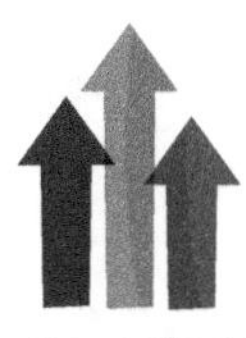

Re-orient

Effective journeys go beyond the simple question of "Are we there yet?" to the powerful questions of "How far have we gone?" and "What will it take to finish the journey?" This step is the action step after the pause to reset the picture of what? where? when? and how? with the most critical step to assign or reassign the who? involved. As roles and tasks shift on a journey, it is important for all teams and individuals to have clarity and alignment on the work ahead. Reorient makes sure that happens.

There are four things that will obstruct your journey and cause it to fail, either through an inability to see, missed steps, or ignoring others on your journey. I call these clouds, and they come in four forms:

Ego: Too much or too little is the issue here. The key signs are statements like, "They can't..." or "They won't..."

Fear: It either has a paralyzing effect or causes you to make big, quick, and often reckless decisions without considering any input from others.

Self-doubt: It can sound a lot like too little Ego, but the biggest challenge is getting people to speak up and share. This cloud causes people to disappear.

Crisis thinking: It is often rooted in fear, and moves decision-making to the amygdala or, as Seth Godin calls it, 'The Lizard Brain'. This is most commonly called the 'fight-or-flight' response.

Visit thetrugroup.com/honest-culture-journey to learn more about the tools I have created to equip you for this journey and to get on a list to hear more.

www.ingramcontent.com/pod-product-compliance
Lightning Source LLC
LaVergne TN
LVHW081255100826
845148LV00009B/1225

* 9 7 8 1 7 3 3 1 3 4 6 3 7 *